THE RELUCTANT COOK

THE RELUCTANT COOK

A JOURNEY TO APPRECIATING SIMPLE GOOD FOOD

E. BENTINCK

PHILIP GREER PUBLICATIONS

First published in 2011 by

Philip Greer Publications

Woodside, Lochearnhead, FK19 8QD

Copyright © E. A. Greig 2011

The right of E. A. Greig to be identified as the author of this work has been asserted by her in accordance with the Copyright, Designs and Patents Act, 1988.

All rights reserved. No part of this publication may be reproduced, stored, or transmitted in any form, or by any means, electronic, mechanical, or photocopying, recording or otherwise, without the express written permission of the publisher.

To Miss Bewick

and with many thanks to my family and to Belinda Buxton

ISBN 978-0-9523384-1-3

Typeset by Cobalt Violet (Media), Edinburgh Ltd.

Printed and bound by CPI Group (UK) Ltd, Croydon, CR0 4YY

CONTENTS

Chapter 1
Cook's Journey   07

Chapter 2
Equipment   25
Lunches   Sandwiches   29
                Soups   30
Main Meals   Meat   34
                Fish   42
Vegetarian   44
Puddings   48

Chapter 3
Bonus Meals   51

Chapter 4
Entertaining   63
Picnics and Camping   73
Healthy Eating   77

Chapter 5
Baking   83

Chapter 6
Cooking with heat storage cookers   91
And a little bit of self-sufficiency   92

The Reluctant Cook

Chapter One

These days we are told to tighten our belts, not waste food, not buy ready meals – cook your own, make your own clothes, grow your own vegetables. All this must seem very difficult to anyone under the age of sixty. Since I have never done anything else I suddenly find myself in a prime position of knowing exactly how to do all these things – great, except that I am not going to gain any savings as I do them already.

I was brought up during rationing – there was very little meat but there were lots of vegetables grown by my mother. She became an accomplished cook, making delicious meals out of very little. She had learnt simple cooking as a Girl Guide, and how to make a little go far, from living in a Highland manse as one of ten children.

Cooking never entered my head. It was not taught at school, I did not cook at home – I did not even like eating. Meals were something to be endured. I was even treated for malnutrition – perhaps that is what they call anorexia now. The

The Reluctant Cook

French Camping

one food I remember enjoying was fritters – a good way to make a little cheese, bacon or vegetables go further.

In the late 1940s, just after the end of the second world war, my parents took myself and two brothers on camping trips in Europe visiting war-time friends who had returned to their homes. We travelled in an ancient Rover which constantly broke down and could only get up a hill if we all, except my father the driver, got out and walked. Restrictions on foreign exchange meant we could take very little money abroad. An old trunk on the car roof contained our clothes, basic camping equipment, tinned food and sugar (saved from our rations) which my mother sometimes exchanged for bread and milk. We mostly slept in the tent but occasionally we stayed and ate in small inns. Always four meals and five plates were ordered. Not expected to eat much I made do with bits off the other plates. Considering this a gross unfairness I began to show an interest in the food – fish with strange herbs and vegetables – different breads and cheeses and most memorable of all –

stuffed tomatoes. The large sun grown tomatoes would have tasted much better than the ones at home. We always began these holidays with my mother's Medley pie – produced at the first picnic and eagerly anticipated as a great start to the holiday. Shortcrust pastry was filled with mince, boiled eggs, peas, green beans, tomato and potato.

By the early 1950s any family celebration meant a meal out using the newly founded Good Food Club guide. I began to appreciate good food – good ingredients simply cooked either at home or out. I still have a 1954 edition of Raymond Postgate's Good Food Guide and it is interesting to see what you could get then. Dinner at the first class George Hotel in Edinburgh cost 8s 6d – sole and lobster on the menu – whilst the Café Royal, still in the current book, served excellent grilled fish from 3s 6d.

Despite this new interest in food I never intended to be a cook. A planned Fine Arts course at the Courtauld Institute collapsed due to a change in family circumstances. From improving my bad French at a Swiss University (languages were a course requirement) I had to hurry home to move my family of three ill people from London back to Scotland. Once we were settled into an old Edinburgh manse my mother, now very ill, sensibly realised that the comfort of the family would be much improved if the one able-bodied person had some domestic training. She remembered her sister had done a course at the Edinburgh College of Domestic Science or 'Atholl Crescent' as it was generally called from its location – and persuaded the college to take me immediately although I was below the required age. Fine Arts was not mentioned and the course seemed a good idea. I had a large house and three sick people to look after. Having successfully avoided any useful domestic knowledge at school by doing extra art and music, I was hopelessly ill-equipped to care for them.

Overladen with white and green overalls, vast white aprons and an impressive set of knives (worth several Asbos) I cycled across Edinburgh in a freezing East wind anxious to learn enough to make my life easier and to enjoy a break from the house. Behind the elegant façade of a New Town crescent the college was a warren of well polished corridors, lecture rooms and kitchens. My classroom appeared cold and unwelcoming. White walls, white uniforms and white cookers and fridges. Frozen I made for the only welcoming item – a black solid fuel range. It must have been there since the college began, and with its cheerful glow and comforting warmth it was much more appealing than the newest gas and electric cookers over which the rest of the class were squabbling. We were told to choose a cooker in pairs but there was only one other taker for my choice and J. and I remain friends today. The advantages of our chosen stove were many. First it kept us warm and cheerful. We did not have to wait for it to heat up. We were blissfully ignorant of its main disadvantage – refuelling and clearing out the ashes as this was done for us mostly unseen in the early morning by a kindly janitor. It was of course unpredictable – unlike a modern Aga – and everyone pitied us. But we had a marvellous excuse for our sunken cakes and burnt or undercooked casseroles. It soon became clear we

The Reluctant Cook

Learning to Cook

were the dunces in a class of perfect cooks. No-one else was a complete beginner and one was so accomplished she was recommended when a Royal Household required a cook.

Although the college had kept up with the latest gas and electric cookers and other domestic appliances, it still kept the old ways going. So I learnt to cook on a black lead range, and to iron using flat irons heated on the stove. I expect they believed in the late 1950s – early 1960s we might find ourselves

The Reluctant Cook

in unmodernised houses, and I certainly found the experience useful later when looking after two delightful elderly ladies in just such a house in Cramond.

Life grew much easier at home as I learnt efficient ways of cleaning the house, how to cook tempting dishes for the invalids, and simple basic nursing skills. It grew a little more difficult again during our six weeks' work experience. Day students were accommodated with the boarders, but I had dispensation because of my dependants. I left home at 5 am and bicycled to college in time to lay fires and clean, cook breakfast for 100, or wait on the other students and staff according to the block of duties to which I was assigned. During the afternoon time off I cycled home to see to the invalids and put a casserole in the oven, wash clothes etc. before returning to the college to cook supper, wait on the students or act as kitchen or parlour maid.

If I felt overworked I could read the small booklet written by my paternal great grandmother for her kitchen and parlour maids in 1868. Rising at 5am, apart from all the usual housework, cleaning boots, bringing in coals, as they lived on a Scottish farm their duties included attending to the cows, calves, poultry, dogs and pigs, churning the milk and keeping the white riding and driving harnesses clean. Mondays were particularly bad as they had to rise between 3 and 4 o'clock for washing day. They had to attend morning and evening worship – surely a welcome moment of calm. They must have been ready for the compulsory 10.30pm bedtime.

The Reluctant Cook

J. and I quickly divided the cooking between us as best suited our meagre talents. I did most of the baking and stews and she did the steak and chop cooking. We kept to this plan when we later worked together so I never learnt to fry or grill good meat which mattered little as I could not afford them anyway.

We scraped through our exams – I narrowly missed failing Large Scale Catering because I did not colour the gooseberry fool green and then stupidly defended my objection to colouring. Through friends I was offered a job with a large family on a West Coast island. My mother, wishing me to have a break as a carer, organised my second brother on vacation from university to stay in the house for the summer freeing me to go. J agreed to join me and we set off in her little car full of optimism. The house was in a glorious position overlooking a beautiful sandy beach but the kitchen was a little primitive. No fridge, nothing but a small cooker, sink and a paltry collection of kitchen implements.

We soon established a routine of porridge and cooked breakfasts, packed lunches and large teas. Sometimes J would drive to the main island village for vegetables and to buy meat and ask the butcher how best to cook it. Together we tackled dinner for 20 – 25 people. I used my first wages to buy a weighing machine, finding it impossible to bake without one, but was a little disconcerted to find it being used by one of our employer's sons to weigh his new puppy. We realised what hopeless cooks we were – but the family seemed grateful when

The Reluctant Cook

our meals were eatable and unperturbed when our puddings failed to work. Then the younger members of the family came through to the kitchen to try them anyway. Having no fridge was a big problem to us and when game began to appear we reached breaking point. The kitchen was full of venison for which we were running out of ideas. I read that brine was the answer so we filled our bath (sometimes used by others when all the bedrooms were occupied) with salt and water and venison. Luckily no unsuspecting guest chanced on this scenario reminiscent of the acid bath murders.

Lack of equipment was a problem but we learnt to improvise. It was just a pity I was on the floor with a hammer, tackling a lobster (on a tray), when the lady of the house decided to introduce her important guests to the cooks. We had a lot of practice in skinning rabbits and hares, plucking pheasant and grouse and gutting fish. In fact learning to cook in difficult circumstances was extremely useful. I hope the family did not suffer too much. With a constant supply of cream, eggs and butter from the farm it was possible to disguise the worst of our failures with delicious sauces. Vegetables were difficult to get (they came from the mainland) and I wished someone had kept up the walled kitchen garden – which had become just somewhere else for the sheep to graze. I would walk down to the village telephone box at night, dodging the cows in the dark, to ring my mother for recipe ideas all of which were much appreciated by our employers. Reading old letters of the time I see my mother's rice pudding was described as `simply divine` and a birthday cake we made for one of the children (not very successful – the sunken top and poor icing hidden by sprays of fern and flowers) described as a `dream`. A large dinner party began with my mother's asparagus dish with eggs and rice (especially requested by our employer). Later most of my mother's recipes were lost in fire and flood (more of this later) but from an attempt at re-creation I find it makes a good quick supper dish. In those days years of rationing had dulled the palate, and most people were content with simple plain cooking. Wishing to impress we tried Milanaise Soufflé from our Advanced Cookery Recipe book but it failed to set so we substituted mother's coffee rum/brandy whip made from lemon jelly, evaporated milk, instant coffee and rum which was much appreciated.

After this enjoyable job where we learnt how to cook with the minimum of equipment and improvise with recipes when we lacked many ingredients, I soon found I had neither the qualifications nor the experience to get a permanent well paid job. I still had two semi invalids to cook for with little money, so we lived on Scotch broth, pea soup, and herrings which were plentiful and cheap then. I would buy bones to make stock – not so easy now but there are plenty of excellent stock powders available. I also made oatcakes – good with cheese and soup for lunch. It is interesting how food values change. Many years ago salmon was so plentiful farmhands begged their masters not to serve salmon every day. Then salmon became an expensive treat until fish farms made it as cheap as chicken which in my childhood was a special treat. Herring became scarce and in 2009 I noticed the `plat du jour` at an Edinburgh bistro was herring.

The Reluctant Cook

College cooking

I found a job as a kitchen assistant in a small residential college and then when the cook left to get married I took over her post. A little worried as to my ability to cook successfully single handed for a college of 60 – 80, I took up the offer of an old family friend to stay in the convent where she lived and work with the sister in charge of the kitchen. I learnt an enormous amount working all day with Sister Dorothy and was quite happy to retire early to my tiny cell, as did everyone else, to read until sleep took over.

The Reluctant Cook

Cooking and eating with students and staff I found the Large Scale recipes unpalatable. For example the recipe for scrambled eggs included few eggs, watery milk and cornflour which produced a warm blancmange! I looked to home cook books for inspiration. A 1922 copy of Mrs Beeton contained pictures of banquets far beyond my meagre allowance for food, but Marguerite Patten's books seemed perfect. With these, and with the manse, my mother's own and the Atholl Crescent cook books I was able to cook some interesting and economical food for the students. Mutton (from sheep over two years old) was plentiful and cheap in those days and haricot mutton was popular. So was Irish stew. The latter can be made with extra potatoes and carrots if money and meat are in short supply. Bicycling around Edinburgh in the freezing wind I would sometimes buy myself a comforting hot Scotch pie (made with mutton). Nowadays I make my own version of this using lamb mince if there is no mutton available.

This was an enjoyable job as I was in sole charge of choosing the menus and ordering the food. On my day off a local fisherman's wife deep fried fish and chips for lunch - so no frying or grilling for me! A great deal of baking was needed as high tea was padded out with scones and cakes to fill up the students and once a week there was an open house tea party – anyone could come to a free tea so they were very popular. My assistants, who came from Holland, Germany, Switzerland and Austria to learn English, were my age and we had a jolly time in the kitchen playing classical music on a small gramophone as we worked. During the college holidays we would cycle or walk through the Highlands, camping or staying in youth

The Reluctant Cook

hostels. They must have enjoyed these trips as some remain friends and still return on holiday. But it was here that I lost the first of my treasured cook books. I had been baking and making fudge until 3 am and was so sleepy I stupidly left my grandmother's manse cook book on the stove when I went to bed. The first girl into the kitchen in the morning, equally sleepy, turned on the grill to make toast without noticing the book. The rest of my cookbooks were ruined years later in the 2 ft of mud that flooded our cottage.

It was all great fun but extremely hard work, I often cooked until 2 or 3am catering for the many parties held. It was also extremely badly paid. Eventually I had to leave in order to earn enough money to pay bills. Cooking in private houses was better paid but rather lonely and I did not enjoy the luxury of expensive cuts and exotic puddings. I had to refer to my pristine copy of the Atholl Crescent Edinburgh Book of Advanced Cookery for recipes for Quenelles, Jugged Hare and Charlotte Russe. I was not very good with these or the grilling and frying of expensive steaks so was relieved to go up North, to a house where I had spent happy holidays, to cook for a friend of my grandmother's whose cook was ill. We were high in the hills and far from shops, but the farm produced milk, cream and eggs and there was plenty of game. Best of all there was a huge extremely productive walled garden and an amiable gardener who would either bring me quantities of fresh fruit and vegetables or allow me to forage for myself. Grandmother's friend loved eating outside despite the unpredictable Scottish weather. If it looked promising, even if the table was laid inside, she would suddenly decide 'yes' – and we would reset

The Reluctant Cook

the whole thing in the garden. No picnic this, a big long dining room table, white linen tablecloth, sparkling glasses and everything set properly. The garden was on a hillside so the view was spectacular. Sometimes the ponies would join us but I do not ever remember having to go inside because of the weather.

When cook recovered I moved to the nearby big house. Here the vast Aga made cooking for the many adults, children and guests easy. Porridge was left in the slow oven overnight. On the much smaller Aga I now cook on I find even the coolest oven is too hot so I bring it to the boil, simmer for 5 minutes and leave it on the hob beside the rings overnight. Porridge is a wonderful, cheap, nutritious, filling breakfast. Even if you do not have a solid fuel cooker, bringing it to the boil, simmering for 5 minutes and then just leaving it overnight will shorten the cooking time in the morning. To make a more luxurious dish – cook with milk and add nutmeg, brown sugar, cream and fresh fruit.

One summer at this house the parents' work commitments and emergency health problems meant that I found myself the lone adult in the household of children – although Granny was nearby for advice. The weather was glorious. I would get up very early, swim in the loch with otters around me, cook casseroles and leave them in the cool oven, pack up sandwiches, cakes and fruit and we would spend the day up the hill usually by a loch for swimming and boating. Joined by young cousins and friends from neighbouring houses

The Reluctant Cook

down the glen there would often be a dozen or so who needed feeding. Steamed puddings were a great favourite, still warm, wrapped in towels they were much appreciated after swimming in the icy loch. We took a couple of sturdy Highland ponies and they were invaluable at the end of the day for tired children – and even for tired small dogs. After large helpings of the waiting casserole, off to bed and everyone always slept extremely well. Many years later, attending a conference, a main speaker was one of the girls now grown up and with a PhD. She joined us for lunch, the organiser hovering in the background wondering if his guest speaker was all right. We were deep in conversation, but not academic. We were reminiscing about taking the ponies over the heather hills to the loch and comforting steam puddings on picnics after swimming.

These idyllic short jobs during school holidays were interspersed with less enjoyable work. Once again I was cycling across Edinburgh at 5 am in an icy Edinburgh winter, to cook in a childrens' home. Very low pay and very long hours meant few people stayed long. The final straw was when we were told we had to pay to eat the meals we were cooking. I overcame that problem by using a very large tasting spoon! I did not enjoy cooking the best ingredients for the staff but the poorest quality for the children. The job convinced me finally that catering meant unsociable hours and no social life. It was time to seek other employment.

Although I eventually found much better paid work in offices I hated being shut inside and missed the diversity of my

The Reluctant Cook

former jobs. Then every day was different and there was the challenge of producing something for people to enjoy – a sense of achievement.

After I got married it seemed very easy to cater for just two then three then four. I was determined our two sons would be competent cooks before they left home. They started cooking early – a useful entertainment on dark winter days. A disabled friend of our eldest son meant some games were difficult but cooking was something they could enjoy together. Shepherd's pie for their supper, biscuits, dropped scones and fudge were popular. We managed to salvage Great Granny's recipe from the burnt manse cookbook. Both sons worked at local hotels to earn money on holiday from school and later as students, but by this time I had tried to write down helpful things to aid them in their student flats. Now that they have left home my cooking aims are simple. Cheap healthy meals using the best ingredients I can afford and the simplest of recipes that leave me more time to garden, paint, climb hills, swim, go steamboating and generally enjoy life. For entertaining I am still experimenting with meals that can have the most work done in advance without jeopardizing the quality of the food. I do not want to be worrying about last minute cooking while the guests are enjoying interesting talk, unlike a friend who can cook the most perfect scallops whilst entertaining her waiting guests. I am easily distracted by people chatting to me in the kitchen and guests do not want their hostess to be slaving over a hot stove.

The Reluctant Cook

This book is not about impressing your friends with great dishes. This book is about day-to-day cooking using fresh ingredients – cooking with the minimum effort and cost. Doing this most of the time leaves more money available to spend on enjoying a meal out, buying the occasional frozen meal to use when you are too busy or too stressed to cook, or buying expensive cuts of meat for a treat or for entertaining your friends. Busy lives leave people less time to spend in the kitchen but even using a few of the following ideas will be healthy, save money and even sometimes time. There are plenty of cook books for more exciting recipes and party food. Remember tastes differ so be careful in choosing your book. Make sure you like the author's style of cooking. If possible try a recipe, often some are published in newspapers and magazines or maybe a good friend will tell you which cook book she used for that delicious dish she has just given you. Personally I do not like food which has been handled a lot during preparation – such as dishes where it is arranged in tiers on the plate, a popular fashion at present. Nor do I like anything described as 'warm' or 'wilted'. Food should be hot or cold – warm suggests an ideal climate for bugs to reproduce.

Most people like to eat simple meals, perfectly roasted or grilled meat with fresh lightly cooked vegetables or a well dressed salad, (often Chef's favourite meal when asked). But this style does not sell cookery books nor is it exciting enough for most restaurants. Before the age of ready meals delivered by vans, many pubs and small hotels produced simple meals of good soup, roast local lamb, chicken, ham and fish, and real fruit puddings. Innovative chefs in good restaurants put their

The Reluctant Cook

own mark on the food style of the moment. Chef owners produce wonderful food for a while but find it difficult to keep up the standard day after day unless they can find good staff to support them. They need paying well so prices can be high. Alongside superb, first class restaurants we need less pretentious food with lower prices. Gradually this kind of simpler food is appearing. Recently, while walking the Pennine Way in the North of England, we came across an inn which, although isolated, is very popular: it serves very simple, perfectly cooked fresh food such as roasts and steak and kidney pudding. There is also an excellent popular French Bistro in our nearest town which has never yet failed to provide us with unpretentious delicious simple food.

The Reluctant Cook

Chapter 2

This part of the book was originally written to help students cook cheaply for themselves.

To start at the beginning – a vast amount of equipment is not necessary. Having started cooking with the minimum I soon learnt which were the really essential items:–

A good strong food mixer and liquidiser that can get on with mixing while you are doing other things (not suggested for impoverished students).

A small hand whisk which can be used to rescue lumpy sauces and for mixing in additions to pots on the stove. I still have my mother's cog-handled whisk, invaluable for extremely lumpy sauces or beating cream or egg whites which are easy to overbeat electrically, but a small hand whisk will work just as well.

Essential tools

A stainless steel flat grater. I have had the same one for 40 years. It works perfectly and is easy to clean – much better than all the attachments on my first food mixer which took ages to put together and longer to clean.

A variety of good knives and chopping boards. I cut small amounts of raw meat on a large plate which is easily cleaned. For large amounts of meat, game and fish I use wooden boards, kept solely for this purpose, so that the knife does not slip. Vegetables are chopped on plastic chopping boards which I replace frequently as they soon get worn. Note that raw meat and fish are kept entirely separate from all other food.

A weighing machine. Given five spring balance weighing machines for wedding presents which all broke before long, I bought an old fashioned pair of scales with a set of imperial weights and a set of metric ones. This has worked perfectly for years. If you do not have a weighing machine the following quantities are useful.

1 heaped tablespoon of rice	= 1oz(25g)
2 heaped tablespoons of pasta	= 1oz(25g)
1 heaped tablespoon of sugar	= 1oz(25g)
3 level tablespoons of flour	= 1oz(25g)
1 level tablespoon of butter	= 1oz(25g)

Quantities per person – roughly.

Pasta and rice – 3 to 4oz(75g to 100g)

Most recipe books say 4oz(100g) of meat or fish is needed per person but this can be expensive. Use slightly less and pad a meal out with vegetables, beans, lentils etc. which are cheap, filling and nutritious. Eating cheaply means buying raw ingredients and taking time to put them together. Try to avoid ready cooked and processed meals. Frozen meals are better when you are short of time as they do not contain lots of preservatives. Making your own is nearly always much cheaper and tastes better too.

The Reluctant Cook

How to avoid food poisoning.

1. Make sure frozen chicken is completely defrosted before cooking. Chicken when cooked properly should have a clear juice when pierced with a knife. The juice should not be pink.

2. Do not use the knife and chopping board that you have used to cut up raw meat and fish to cut up things you are not going to cook such as salads. Always wash board and knife immediately after cutting meat. Wash hands too.

3. Keep raw and cooked foods covered and apart in the fridge. It is important to keep raw meat on the bottom shelf so any drips will not contaminate other foods.

4. Do not eat green potatoes – they are poisonous. Keep potatoes in the dark – light turns them green.

5. Put cooked foods you are not eating immediately in fridge or freezer as soon as they are cold.

6. Do not refreeze defrosted food – but you can freeze defrosted raw meat as long as you cook it first – as in a casserole.

7. Wash tea cloths daily.

Breakfast

Many people just want a mug of tea or coffee as they rush to get ready for the day. But a simple breakfast will keep you going till lunch time. Porridge can be prepared the night before. For one bring ½ pint(300ml) water to the boil. Sprinkle in 1 tablespoonful of oatmeal stirring well with a spurtle (carved wooden rod made and used only for porridge) or wooden spoon to avoid lumps. Boil and stir for 5 minutes then with a lid on simmer for 20 minutes. Heat up gently in the morning with a little milk and salt.

Take a little time to make a packed lunch. Sandwiches and rolls with cheese or ham can be frozen for mornings when time is short. We have just finished the last of a batch of home baked cheese rolls left over from a ceilidh. Taken from the freezer two at a time and heated in the oven they were delicious. I try to keep a pack of sandwiches in the freezer for last minute picnics or busy days. I always have a selection of soups for the same reason.

Lunch

I make batches of soup and freeze in small amounts which we have at home with oatcakes and interesting things on bread – I put required number of slices of bread (toast first or spread lightly with butter, margarine or oil) on a baking tray and add one of the following combinations:-

- Sardines and tomato.
- Peanut butter, chopped celery, grated cheese and pumpkin seeds,
- Tomato, chopped celery and pepper, grated cheese and pine nuts or other seeds.

- Chopped celery, sesame seeds, pumpkin seeds, a little olive oil and turmeric.
- Canned mackerel or trout mashed with a little butter and grated cheese. Add chopped spring onions and a little horseradish.
- Basil leaves, sliced tomato, seasoning a sprinkling of oil, pinenuts and grated cheese.
- Cooked broad beans or peas mashed with olive oil. Stir in chopped mint, grated cheese, seasoning and a little lemon juice – spread on toast.
- Spread some red pesto on the bread and cover with chopped mushrooms and spring onions. Add some sunflower seeds and seasoning.

These go in the oven for 10 to 15 minutes. I expect they would be just as good under a grill.

Soups

Pea soup

There are several ways of making pea soup.

Firstly and quickly with fresh or frozen peas. Delicious but be careful not to cook too long and loose the colour.

The Reluctant Cook

1 onion
2 garlic cloves   } all chopped
½ cucumber

½ a lettuce – a good way to use a sad one
½lb(225g) or more frozen peas
fresh mint leaves
1pint(600ml) stock

Cook onion in a little oil and butter, add garlic and cook a little more then add the peas, cucumber and shredded lettuce. Stir well and add stock, half the chopped mint and seasoning. Bring to the boil and simmer for about 3 minutes. Serve at once with the rest of the chopped mint. It will loose its colour if kept, but can be frozen.

More often in the winter I make **split pea soup** – deliciously warming and comforting in cold weather. Easy to make as long as you remember to soak the peas the night before.

6oz(175g) split peas – put in a bowl and cover with water the night before.
1 onion chopped
2 garlic cloves chopped
1 bacon rasher (optional)
2pints(1.2litres) stock

Cook the bacon rasher in a little oil, remove and cook the onion. Cut up the bacon small and replace in the pan with the cooked onion. Add the garlic and the split peas (drained and rinsed). Stir well and add enough stock to cover well. Bring to the boil, season and simmer for 1½ to 2 hours. This is easy in a solid fuel stove or an electric slow casserole cooker. Serve with fresh chopped mint, and adding chopped smoked sausage will turn it into a meal.

If short of time and fresh supplies use canned green peas. Chop onion and fry in butter. Add peas and about ¾ pint (450ml) stock. Bring to the boil and simmer for 5 minutes. Chopped celery, grated carrot or vermicelli can be added to make more of a meal.

Lentil soup – much the same soup as split pea.
    1 rasher bacon chopped (easier to cook first as above)
    1 onion chopped
    1 carrot chopped
    1 stick celery chopped
    1 tin of tomatoes
    6oz(175g) lentils
    2pints(1.2litres) stock and seasoning
    1 small teaspoon cumin seeds (optional extra)

Method as for split pea soup.

Minestrone

- 1 rasher bacon chopped
- 1 stick celery chopped
- 1 carrot chopped or grated
- 1 onion and 2 cloves of garlic chopped
- 1 tin of chopped tomatoes
- 1 – 2 tablespoons of rice
- cabbage, thinly shredded
- chopped herbs (parsley, thyme, rosemary)
- 1 bay leaf
- grated cheese.
- 2pints(1.2litres) stock and seasoning

As above, cook the bacon and onions in a little oil. Add garlic, celery and carrot and stir well, cook a little then add tin of tomatoes. Continue cooking while stirring, then add stock and bring to the boil. Season. Add rice – white rice will take about 15 minutes to cook – brown rice takes about 35 minutes. Cover and simmer for about 35 minutes. Shortly before it is ready add the cabbage and the herbs. Serve with grated cheese.

Barley soup

- 2pints(1.2litres) chicken stock
- 4oz(100g) barley
- 2 tablespoons oil
- 2 onions   chopped
- 2 cloves garlic   "

2 celery stalks
2 carrots   }all chopped
2 potatoes
1 small piece of turnip
seasoning
milk

Fry the onion and garlic in the oil. Stir in the chopped vegetables and the barley (rinsed in cold water). Add the stock and seasoning – bring to the boil and simmer for 1 – 1½ hours. Add a little milk and chopped parsley before serving.

Other vegetable soups

Experiment with whatever vegetables you have left. Beetroot, onion and carrot make a delicious and cheering red soup. Parsnip goes particularly well with a little mild curry powder. Chopped or shredded green vegetables (cabbage, broccoli, leeks, kale or brussels sprouts) can be added to soups shortly before serving.

Main meals

Steaks and chops are the obvious quick meal. I like Edouard de Pomiane's 10 - minute dinner party for a friend, from his book Cooking in 10 minutes first published in 1948.

I have tried this using a lamb chop and frozen peas and

The Reluctant Cook

it works perfectly. The kettle goes on for coffee later, then mix the dressing for salad and make an omelette (with herbs, tomato, and cheese) while the chops are quickly fried in hot butter and oil on both sides. Eat the omelette while the chops gently cook at a lower temperature with the added peas. Eat these with the salad and, with some cheese, apple, and coffee to follow, you have a banquet that took little time or trouble to make.

But good cuts of meat are expensive – cheaper cuts do make delicious casseroles. People are put off cooking the more economical dishes because they take a long time. Stews may take 2 hours to cook but you don't need to be there. You just have to think ahead. I usually cook a proper Sunday lunch so while doing that I quickly put together a large casserole which can simmer gently. (This also has the advantage making use of the oven when it is on.) When cold I freeze the casserole in small quantities for quick meals during the week.

Some simple main meals are worth making too much of as they will provide the basis for several other meals.

Mince

    1lb(450g) mince (buy the best you can afford)
    1 onion
    2 cloves garlic
    1 dessert spoon of flour
    1 tablespoon of oil

Fry chopped onion and 2 cloves of garlic in oil then add mince and beat out any lumps as it browns. Sprinkle in the flour and stir well. Add stock to cover it, and seasoning. Bring to the boil stirring and simmer for 1 hour. To this basic recipe add any of the following:

Sliced mushrooms fried with the onion, a tin of chopped tomatoes and mixed herbs –rosemary, thyme and bay leaf, and a small glass of red wine will turn it into a Bolognese sauce to go over rice. Serve with grated cheese.

Chopped carrot, celery and a tin of beans (baked, haricot or kidney) will help to feed more people. Add peas and parsley just before serving.

Stew

 1lb(450g) stewing beef
 2 tablespoonfuls oil
 1oz(25g) flour
 1pint(600ml) stock
 1 onion
 1 carrot   }all chopped
 2 sticks celery

Make the oil hot enough in the pan for the meat to sizzle when it goes in. Brown the meat quickly – do this in batches a few at a time and lift out onto a plate. Then fry the onion until browned. Sprinkle in the flour and cook a little, then add the stock and bring to the boil, stirring. Add meat, vegetables and seasoning and simmer for 1½-2 hours. To make this meal go further add herb dumplings 20 minutes before serving.

Dumplings
    4oz(100g) self raising flour
    2oz(50g) suet
    seasoning
    about 5 tablespoons of water
    chopped mixed herbs

Mix all together well and add enough water to make a workable dough. Flour hands and make about 8 balls – put on top of bubbling stew – cover and cook for 20 minutes.

Steamed steak
    1 lb(450g) stewing beef
    1 large onion, 1 carrot and 2 celery sticks chopped
    parsley and seasoning
    stock

Fry the meat quickly in a little oil – take out and fry the sliced onion. In an earthenware pot or jar layer the meat and chopped vegetables seasoning as you do so. Just cover with hot stock. Cover tightly with a well fitting lid. Place pot in a pan of boiling water and steam for 3 hours. I put the pan in the top oven of the Aga for 30 minutes and then in the bottom oven for the rest of the time. Thicken the stew with flour blended with stock and continue simmering for 15 minutes. Add chopped parsley. The meat is very tender and delicious. This dish could also now be cooked in an electric slow cooker. It was a useful way to cook stew on an open fire for the many Highland guide camps my mother attended with her sisters after the First World War. There is a similar recipe called Hunter's Stew in her copy of Miss Baden Powell's Handbook for Guides.

Irish stew

    2 chops
    1 large onion
    2 potatoes
    2 carrots
    1 stick celery
    stock and seasoning

    This is included as a way to make 2 lamb chops go much further. In a casserole (ring proof as well as oven proof) put a layer of sliced potato, then a layer of sliced onion. Next place the two small chops, season, add chopped carrot and celery and more onion and potato continuing until the casserole is almost full. Finish with a layer of sliced potato. Half fill the dish with boiling water/stock – bring to the boil, cover and cook in a slow oven for about 2 hours. Remove the lid and brown the top either in a hot oven for about 15 minutes or under a grill.

Any left over can be used to make Scotch Broth. Add extra vegetables, stock and 2 tablespoons of Broth mixture (barley, split peas, lentils etc. – soak overnight) for every 1 pint (600 ml) of stock. Serve with chopped parsley.

Scottish Pie (my version of a Scotch Pie)
10oz(245g) lamb mince (if not enough meat, add cooked haricot beans)
1 onion
2 cloves of garlic
2oz(50g) barley
1 stick celery
1 carrot
small piece of turnip
stock to cover meat
rosemary
parsley
a spoonful of flour

Fry chopped onion and garlic in a little oil – add mince and brown carefully beating out any lumps. Add chopped carrot and barley. Sprinkle in flour and stir to cook it. Add stock and seasoning and simmer 1 hour. Add chopped herbs and celery.

Pastry

    4oz(100g) fat

    8oz(200g) flour (try a mixture of barley, oatmeal and malt flour)

    pinch of salt and approx 3 tablespoons of cold water

Rub the fat into the flour and salt. Mix in the water to make a ball of dough which can be halved then rolled out on a floured board.

Line a greased baking dish with pastry and put in meat. Cover with pastry and cook for ½ hour in a hot oven.

Roast Chicken

Chickens usually come with cooking instructions and timings according to their weight. Put an onion or lemon inside the carcass. Place two bacon rashers on the chicken, season, scatter some chopped herbs and dot with butter or drizzle a little oil over the top. Cover lightly with a piece of foil. Roast in a hot oven, removing the foil about 15 minutes before it is ready to brown the top.

To make soup from the roast chicken, when all the best meat has been removed from the bones put in a pan and add 2 pints of cold water, a carrot, onion, bay leaf, seasoning and parsley (stalks are fine). Add any scraps of chicken and the bacon. Bring slowly to the boil and skim off the foam. Simmer for 1 to 2 hours, strain and leave to cool. Remove any fat from top. This stock can then be used to make chicken soup (see Soups) or with milk as a sauce with chicken (see Bonus meals).

Boiled Chicken

Even easier is boiled chicken. A friend who contracted TB in her youth and had frequent stretches in bed throughout a long life always made sure of a boiled chicken to sustain her. Easy to cook and providing soup, meat and vegetables.

Put the chicken in a large pan with 1 carrot and 1 onion, sliced. Add a bay leaf, parsley and thyme and seasoning. Bring slowly to the boil, skim off any foam and simmer for 1 hour. This method of cooking was formally used to make tender old chickens which would need 2 to 3 hours simmering. A sauce can be made from the liquor and a little milk – add lots of fresh chopped herbs. The rest can be used for soup.

Boiled ham

Cover with cold water and bring slowly to the boil, skim well and simmer until tender (25minutes per lb(450g)). Twenty five minutes before it is ready add pieces of carrot, potato and celery and you have a meal in one pan made with the minimum of effort. Add plenty of chopped herbs and some peas before serving. With most of the guests gone, after a week of feasting on Italian food and wine our hostess produced this simple dish which perfectly suited our mood and palates.

Fish

The ultimate quick meal – fried, grilled or baked in the oven. I do not do deep frying. Why bother with all the problems with large amounts of oil? Of course the fish oil cannot be used again for anything else – no doughnuts for the children. You need a large pan and there is always the fear of overheating, bubbling over and fire. I would rather leave it to a good fish and chip shop.

To fry - coat fillets in a little seasoned flour, then 1 beaten egg and finally in breadcrumbs. Heat some oil and a little butter in a pan and fry from 2 to 6 minutes on each side depending on the thickness of the fish. For example sole 2 minutes a side and thick fish steaks like cod could take up to 6 minutes a side.

Baking.

Either put the ingredients in a dish and cover lightly with foil or put the fish inside a parcel of foil so retaining all the juices.

White fish

1. Butter an ovenproof dish – put in fish. Cover with chopped mushroom, pepper, tomato and seasoning and dot with a little butter. Cover with foil and bake for about 25 minutes. After 20 minutes you could remove the foil and scatter some grated cheese.

The Reluctant Cook

2. Place 2 fillets in an ovenproof dish (add a boiled egg if short of fish.) Make a sauce with 1oz(25g) butter cooked gently with 1oz(25g) flour. Add 1/2pint(300ml) milk slowly, stirring until bubbling. Season, stir in chopped spinach or watercress and pour over fish. Instead of boiling the eggs could be added raw at this stage. Add tomatoes and mushrooms. Scatter grated cheese and cook for twenty minutes in a hot oven.

Salmon is good sealed in a foil parcel with a little butter, seasoning and dill.

Experiment with ingredients . Try a selection from onion, garlic, parsley, white wine, celery, basil, lemon, bacon, bay leaves, thyme. Evolve your own great dishes.

There is plenty in the press about overfishing and the consequent declining stocks of some fish. Cod, haddock, herring, halibut and tuna are all in trouble. We should try to eat fish from sustainable stocks. Buy from a knowledgeable fishmonger if you are lucky enough to have one near. Supermarkets are giving much more information on packaging now. For example saying if the contents are line caught, which is better than trawling for cod, whiting or haddock. Look out for the Logo of the Marine Stewardship Council (fish with tick on blue oval) indicating environmentally responsible fisheries. Supermarkets also say where the fish is caught.

People are suspicious of unusual fish names and would rather stick to familiar cod and haddock. But there are plenty of good alternatives. Dabs are similar to plaice and pollock is similar to cod. Coley is also similar to cod but best used for pies or soup. Try also red mullet, sea bass and trout.

Fish is the ultimate quick meal.

Vegetarian meals

Stuffed peppers
> 2 peppers
> 3oz(75g) mushrooms
> 1 small onion
> 2 cloves garlic
> 2oz(50)g lentils
> 4oz(100g) millet
> ½pint(300ml) stock
> seasoning
> 1 to 2oz(25 – 50g) pine nuts and or pumpkin seeds
> 2 tomatoes
> oil and a little butter
> optional extra – add a dessertspoon of red pesto to the stuffing.

Halve the peppers and remove seeds. Brush with oil and put in a dish in a hot oven for 20 minutes. Meanwhile, to make the stuffing: sauté chopped onion and garlic in oil. Add chopped mushrooms, stir in well with the millet and lentils. Add stock, bring to the boil and simmer for 15 to 20 minutes. Add the pine nuts/pumpkin seeds (briefly roasted in the oven – careful they burn easily). Add the chopped mint or parsley. Season, mix well and put the stuffing into the pepper halves. Top with half a tomato, seasoning and a small bit of butter. Add a little water to the dish and replace in the oven for 15 to 20 minutes. Serve with broad beans in a herb sauce made with thickened liquor from cooking the beans and a little milk. Add a mixture of herbs, chopped parsley, thyme, rosemary and /or marjoram. If there is too much stuffing it can be tossed with chopped celery and added to the plate.

Courgette, couscous and avocado

Sauté 1 chopped onion and 2 cloves of garlic in a little oil and butter. Add 2 chopped courgettes and cook slowly for a few minutes. Just before serving add a little cream/top of the milk, chopped mixed herbs and seasoning,

Cook the couscous (as packet instructions.) Add mixed seeds and nuts of choice (sesame, pine nuts, pumpkin seeds, sunflower seeds) chopped celery and spring onions, herbs and seasoning and sprinkle with some grated cheese.

Chop stoned and peeled avocado and 2 tomatoes and toss in French dressing (add 1/2 teaspoon mustard and a sprinkling of tumeric). Add shredded lettuce and chopped mint or parsley just before serving. Alternatively serve chopped tomato, red pepper and celery tossed in a dressing of 1 teaspoon balsamic vinegar, 1 dessert spoon olive oil, seasoning and a little sugar. Add basil and lettuce just before serving. Tricky to get everything ready together but it does not take long and is worth the effort.

Belinda's Meal for Hungry Students

Serves 4 - 6

    1 bag of pasta 1lb(450g)

    2 large onions

    2 cloves of garlic

    2 tins of chopped tomatoes

    2 eggs

    olive oil

    4oz(100g) grated cheese - herbs – oregano or basil

Cook pasta for 12 minutes. Chop onions and garlic and fry in oil. (Extra option – mushrooms, celery.) Add tomatoes and stir as sauce thickens. Remove pan from heat and stir in beaten eggs, herbs and cooked drained pasta. Stir well – sprinkle cheese on top and grill.

The Reluctant Cook

Belinda's student meal is exactly what it says – a good cheap filling dish. For two people I made half the recipe, which we might have found too much if we had not spent the day building a jetty. It was a good quick warming supper for cold tired people.

Sunday evening supper

For a light supper I cook cauliflower or broccoli or fennel and potato until just tender, then make a light sauce from a little butter, sprinkling of flour and the vegetable cooking liquor to which I have added a spoonful of dried milk. Stir in a little fresh milk and pour over the vegetables arranged in a shallow dish. Add extras such as 2 rows of sliced courgettes, halved tomatoes, mushrooms, or add some asparagus tossed in oil or melted butter after 10 minutes. Season and sprinkle with pumpkin seeds and grated cheese and bake in a hot oven for about 20 minutes.

Stuffed tomatoes

Cut off the tops of two tomatoes and scoop out centre. Season the inside of the tomato. Fry ½ chopped onion in butter, add two chopped mushrooms and chopped garlic clove. Stir in approx. two tablespoons of breadcrumbs and chopped herbs (any of parsley, basil, thyme, marjoram, rosemary). Fill the tomatoes with the mixture (if it is too dry add a little of the tomato juice removed earlier). Dot with butter and bake for about 10 – 15 minutes in a hot oven. Any leftover mixture can be spread on mushrooms and cooked together.

Puddings

Eves pudding, Manse apple rice, fruit pies and steamed puddings are useful for filling up children and getting some fruit inside them. Children are more likely to eat rhubarb when it is cooked with oranges. We grow raspberries, black and red currants, rhubarb, gooseberries, apples and Worcester berries which everyone hates picking because of their very long thorns. There are plenty of brambles and alpine strawberries which are well worth letting run wild in the garden – as for pudding you can send the children to graze for themselves. Although delicious they are so small it takes a long time to collect enough for a meal. As I write at the end of May there is just enough in the freezer to last until the new seasons fruit is ready. So except for entertaining the puddings we eat are always fruit – with cream sometimes but to be healthier more often with baked custard or rice, or plain yoghurt mixed with cinnamon.

A favourite hill walking picnic portable pudding is gingerbread, cheese and apple. I include one decadent pudding (coffee ice) in the chapter on entertaining. It is useful to have in the freezer as it contains meringue, so that you can easily slice it frozen leaving enough for the next party or sneaky slithers to enjoy with fruit at any time.

Manse Apple Rice

Either oven bake 2 oz(50g) Carolina (pudding) rice with 1 oz(25g) sugar and 1 pint (600ml) milk for about two hours in a moderate oven or boil the same ingredients in a

The Reluctant Cook

Perfect mountain picnic

double saucepan . If using an ordinary pan just cover the rice with cold water and boil without stirring until the water has gone then add the milk and simmer - add sugar when cooked. Or you could just buy a tin of rice pudding!

Chop up a couple of apples – or other fruit - and stir into the rice with the yolk of an egg. Mix well. Beat the white of egg until stiff, fold in a tablespoon of castor sugar and spread over the rice. Cook in a cool oven until the meringue has set softly.

Bread and Butter Pudding

Butter an ovenproof dish approx. 8 x 5ins (20 x 13cm). Place approx, 2oz(50g) frozen fruit mixed with 1 chopped apple on the base of the dish. Beat 1 large egg with 1 dessertspoon of sugar. Add just under 1/4pint(150ml) milk. In this soak 2 quartered, crustless bread slices and place on the fruit. Pour any excess liquid over the top. Drizzle a little melted butter and sprinkle a little brown sugar over the top. Bake for approx. 30 minutes in a hot oven.

Chapter 3

Bonus Meals

Larousse Gastronomique dismisses leftovers as a sign of bad management or poor cooking unless the food is especially prepared in large quantities with the intention of being served again. But this magnificent encyclopaedia is aimed at the professional kitchen not home cooks with small budgets.

I do not want to call them 'leftovers' – That is an unappetising word except after giving a party when you can slump in front of the fire – not needing to cook – feasting on the remains.

If you are not going to use excess food immediately it is a good idea to freeze it rather than leave it in the fridge where it is invariably forgotten – nothing worse than little dishes of festering bits. Do remember you must not refreeze food that has already been frozen and defrosted – unless it was raw and has been cooked since. Put the bits in the door of the freezer or packed separately, clearly labelled together in a large bag, so they do not get lost and are easily found for a quick meal.

Now is the time for experiments. We have a good village shop for essential everyday needs and I can also buy lamb, venison and trout locally but for more unusual ingredients and vegetables it is a 60 mile round trip to a supermarket, so I tend to shop only when I am in town for other things and make do until there are several reasons to waste more petrol. This makes for some interesting new recipes as one jiggles the dwindling supplies. But I enjoy the challenge of making something out of nothing – most satisfying if the result is worth repeating. I love the passage from Elizabeth Goudge's book Castle on the Hill in which Miss Brown, arriving at a crumbling castle desperate for lodging and a job, finds only a mutton bone, a few old carrots and a tired onion with which to impress her new employer. She discovers a neglected vegetable garden and makes soup out of lettuce leaves and milk, stew out of the mutton bone, herbs and vegetables and a pudding from strawberries and egg whites. With this feast Miss Brown impressed not only her employer but his cantankerous butler as well.

Spring is a lean time before the new vegetables are ready. Turnips become tough but as they go to seed I strip off the green leaves and make a sauce which is surprisingly good with meat.

The Reluctant Cook

My mother was not good at passing on her recipes because she did not bother with exact quantities – a handful of this – a sprinkle of that – it worked brilliantly for her but not for me. I kept strictly to exact quantities during my years of cooking for other people but now like her I rarely bother. I use what I have – making every meal different and sometimes more interesting. I try to take note of things that work well together and just wish I had written down the unusual ingredients for the best ever Christmas cake. Start with small amounts and taste often. Trial and error will teach which things combine well and which do not. It was interesting to note at a recent celebration restaurant meal in Edinburgh where you choose your own ingredients from a wide range of meat, fish, herbs and spices etc. – people who cooked knew what to include and what to leave out. Others who chucked in ingredients randomly did not enjoy their meal so much and a dish for the birthday boy where everyone added their chosen ingredient was predictably completely uneatable.

I do follow some recipes loosely but will often reduce quantities of meat and dairy products as in one for chicken in a cheese sauce where I replaced most of the cheese with herbs – the taste was more subtle and much healthier.

The last bacon rasher in the pack, or frozen for later is one of the most useful things there. It can be used for the basis of so many dishes. It is used in some of soup recipes in that section. It can be used as the base for a quick pasta sauce. Cook the bacon in a little oil. Remove and chop up while

The Reluctant Cook

chopped onion and garlic are frying gently in the bacon flavoured oil. Add mushrooms , tomato, celery, peppers, herbs (chopped) – whatever you have available, replace the bacon, sprinkle on a little flour to soak up the juices add stock and you have a sauce ready for the pasta which if you put it on to cook first thing will be ready. Pour sauce over pasta, add grated cheese - a meal in 12 minutes.

For a slightly different sauce cook bacon and onion as above, add chopped mushrooms, courgettes and tomatoes. Cook a little then add 2 tablespoons of crème fraiche and chopped watercress. Serve with boiled rice.

Omelette – Cook the single chopped up bacon rasher in a little oil and butter. Add some leftover vegetables (or lightly cook some diced carrot and potato). When sizzling add 2 beaten, seasoned eggs with a dash of milk and sprinkle on some grated cheese. Mushrooms, tomatoes, raw chopped broccoli and herbs can also be added. This does not make a proper omelette as it is too bulky. Put in the oven for approximately 15 minutes or under the grill to cook the top. Skill is needed to cook a proper omelette – quickly over a high heat. The best I have ever had were cooked to order, while you watched, at a breakfast buffet in a hotel in Vermont, USA .

Recently I needed a quick meal before going out for the evening. Stocks were low – just one leek, a little cheese and some eggs. I strained some onion, garlic and potato from the previous day's soup – sautéed this in butter, added the chopped leek (lightly cooked – the cooking liquor went back into the soup). I beat three eggs, added seasoning, a sprinkling of grated cheese and some raw chopped kale and sprouting broccoli from the garden. Cook for 20 minutes in a hot oven. This was good enough to repeat with fresh cooked onion and potato and raw chopped kale and broccoli.

The bacon rasher could be used in the following chicken and sausage recipes to add flavour but is not essential.

Economical chicken recipe

From two chicken legs I produced two meals for two, soup for two and enough scraps to enliven the dog's meal. Simmer the chicken for 40 minutes in stock /water to cover, with chopped carrot, celery, onion and herbs (bay leaf, rosemary, thyme and parsley). Add potatoes for the last 20 minutes. With fresh mange-tout from the garden we had a meal with the best of meat and a little of the broth. For the next meal add 4oz(100g) green lentils to chopped onion fried in oil. Add ¼pint (150ml) of the chicken broth and a little white wine to cover and simmer for about 30 minutes. Add herbs, chopped leeks and celery towards the end of cooking. Add remnants of chicken. Serve with broad beans in a parsley sauce. Extra vegetables, herbs and a little milk turned the last of the broth into just enough soup for two and a few scraps were enjoyed by the dog.

The Reluctant Cook

Another economical chicken recipe

Simmer the two chicken legs with chopped carrot, onion and herbs (bay leaf, thyme and rosemary) for 40 minutes. Remove the meat from the bones. Sauté chopped onion and garlic in butter and oil – add chopped carrot, parsnip, celery and a small tin of sweetcorn. A dusting of flour and stir in some of the cooking liquor and milk. Add chopped broccoli – more herbs. Cover with partly cooked sliced potatoes and bake in the oven for 20 to 30 minutes. This sauce could also be used with rice or put in pancakes, rolled up and placed in dish and topped with sliced tomatoes and grated cheese and cooked in the oven for 20 to 30 minutes. Pancakes are quick to make and can be frozen so make a batch and you have the basis for another quick meal.

Pancake recipe

    4oz(100g) flour
    1 egg
    ½pint(300ml) milk
    seasoning

Stir the egg and some of the milk into the flour to make a smooth batter. Beat well and add the rest of the milk. Cover and leave to stand for 30 minutes. Put in a jug. Heat oil in a small omelette pan and pour in just enough batter to cover the bottom thinly. Cook until golden brown, shaking gently and easing the sides with a knife. Toss or flip over with the help of a knife.

The Reluctant Cook

This pancake mixture can also be used for fritters but use less milk. Add chopped cooked bacon, chopped herbs, grated cheese, lightly cooked vegetables – leftovers or even a little mince. Fry spoonfuls in hot oil, turning when bubbles appear.

Sausage

Sauté chopped onion and garlic in a little oil. Add chopped pepper, 2 chopped mushrooms and cook for 5 minutes. Then add 2 chopped tomatoes, season and cook slowly for another 5 minutes. Add a little stock if necessary, chopped parsley and the cooked sliced sausage. Make sure it is all piping hot. Serve with hot potatoes tossed in a French dressing (add ½ teaspoonful of mustard or turmeric) and a salad.

Excess sausage could also be chopped and added to pea soup with chopped mint.

Fish

The last one-portion block of frozen fish left in the freezer can be turned into a meal for two. Allow the fish to thaw sufficiently to be able to slice it up. Slice potato and chop onions and celery – carrots too if it does not look as though there is enough food. Add a little milk, seasoning, halved tomatoes and grated cheese on top. Cook for approx. 30 minutes in a moderate oven.

Kedgeree

I buy a packet of two smoked trout or peppered mackerel. I use one fillet for kedgeree and one for the bread topping described earlier.

1 small piece of smoked fish; choose from -
- finnan haddock,
- smoked trout,
- salmon or tinned salmon,
- mackerel
- sardines

4oz(100g brown rice
peas
parsley
1 egg
1 onion

Boil brown rice for 35 minutes (white rice for 15 mins). If using uncooked fish simmer gently in a little milk/water for about 8 minutes. Remove skin and bones and flake. Meanwhile fry chopped onion in butter/oil gently for 5 to 10 minutes. Add flaked fish to onion plus chopped hard boiled egg (10 minutes), drained rice and peas. Season and sprinkle with a little nutmeg. Chopped celery and tomato could also be added. If you are short of fish add extra eggs and a little curry powder to the cooked onions. Serve with salad or buttered, barely cooked shredded cabbage.

Meat

Those small batches of cooked mince in the freezer are useful for all sorts of dishes.

Macaroni mince

Cook macaroni (6oz(175g)) for 12 minutes.

Mix macaroni with cooked mince. Stir well – add chopped celery and any of the following depending on how much mince you have left. Chopped tomatoes, mushrooms and onions (cook these first in a little oil before adding mince and macaroni) grated carrot, chopped raw broccoli, leeks or shredded cabbage. Sprinkle grated cheese on top and put in oven or under grill for about 15 to 20 minutes.

Mince will also make a Bolognese sauce – see recipe earlier

Stuff seasoned tomatoes with a little mince. Top with breadcrumbs and grated cheese and cook in hot oven for about 20 minutes.

Medley Pie

The Medley Pie my mother made to start our holidays, mentioned in the first chapter, contained very little meat, which was rationed. She used potatoes, carrots, beans, peas, tomatoes and parsley from the garden and eggs from our chickens. I made it recently to feed some hungry jetty builders down by the loch.

8oz(225g) plain flour – and a pinch of salt
4oz(100g) butter and 2-3 tablespoons of water to make the pastry.

Line a flan dish with pastry and fill with a little cooked mince or chicken in gravy mixed with 2 chopped boiled eggs, chopped cooked potatoes, carrot and parsley, and some peas. I added chopped lightly cooked mange-tout as the beans are not ready yet.

Use whatever you have – each pie will be different and interesting.

I cooked a drier mince than normal – I did not have any leftovers in the freezer so was starting from scratch so I made 1lb(450g) of mince as in the recipe earlier but used 1 teaspoonful of flour, a tin of chopped tomatoes plus tin rinsed out with just enough water to cover (about ¼pint(150ml)). Cover with pastry and bake for 30 minutes in a hot oven. The rest of the mince was frozen for later meals.

When making pastry the trimmings can be kneaded together, kept in cling film in the fridge and used for a quick snack lunch for two. Roll out the pastry thinly, halve a bacon rasher and place on pastry. Add chopped spring onion, mushroom, tomato and pepper. Season and add sesame, pumpkin or sunflower seed – or pinenuts. Drizzle a little oil over and bake for 20 minutes or so until the bacon and pastry are cooked.

Curry

To leftover lamb/mutton add chopped onion, garlic, dates, apricots, apple, tomato and herbs plus coconut, cinnamon and curry powder to make a simple mild curry.

The Reluctant Cook

The Reluctant Cook

Chapter 4

Entertaining

There are several types of cooking – to keep one alive, for interest (trying new recipes) and cooking for guests. I have no wish now to cook for elaborate dinner parties – aiming for perfection or large parties of 100 or more. Some of the most successful meals were quite simple – they suited the people and place. Friends touring the finest hotels in Scotland said the meal of salmon mousse, beef with horseradish and strawberry shortcake they had with us was the most delicious.

The meal that prompted a delighted employer to bring the cooks a bottle of Drambuie afterwards was very simple – asparagus/egg/rice, goulash and dumplings and fruit meringue. A birthday lochside picnic for a god daughter was pronounced perfect as everyone could choose from a selection of hot soup, cold meats, salmon, home made beefburgers, various salads, fresh baked rolls, oatcakes, cheese and home made ice cream, raspberries and shortcake. There was something for even the pickiest eater. Twelve students who had just successfully traversed the Aonach Eagach (two miles of a high-altitude, steep, rocky, narrow ridge in the Scottish Highlands) were extremely pleased with vast quantities of lasagne, fresh vegetables and Eves pudding.

Then there were the disastrous meals which somehow had to be saved and certainly brought everyone together to produce memorable occasions. As a child we spent Christmas day in hospital where my doctor father dressed up to suit the decorated theme of the ward to carve a turkey which we took round the beds – carefully avoiding those with 'Nil by Mouth' cards – I think those were the first words I learnt to read. Carols were sung, tea was drunk and then home where my mother had been preparing for our Christmas dinner shared with friends. A dozen or more would sit round a large mahogany table which my mother decorated with a magnificent centre piece Christmas scene. One year a very large friend gave a big sigh of appreciation at the beautiful table and blew a candle flame too near the cotton wool snow covered hills. The whole table erupted into flames – fuelled by the French polished table. Disaster was averted by using a rug to smother the fire. Apart from my mother's singed dress and eyebrows no-one was hurt. The food escaped damage and we had a lively dinner eaten among the debris on a heavily scarred table.

Enormous effort went in to organising a 21st birthday party 70 miles from home. Determined that all should run smoothly many lists were made and every step allocated among six people. Nothing could go wrong – but everything did.

The Reluctant Cook

Hospital Christmas

First the frozen casseroles refused to defrost in one of the hardest January frosts in years. Arriving at the venue no chairs had been provided and we were unable to turn on the gas cookers. The music system had not arrived and two of my helpers were ill. Husband and one son set off in search of a replacement music system leaving just two of us to turn an empty room into a party place with dinner for 100. Precious moments were wasted finding chairs and setting up tables. We flung tablecloths and pre-prepared flower arrangements about whilst fruitlessly seeking someone to mend the cookers and trying to find the drinks which should have been delivered. Panic set in as the first guests arrived, thankfully with the drinks which had been sent to the wrong hall. At last we had something to offer people. The first course of cold canapés etc. were served with drinks for a very long time until eventually the cookers were lit and we could serve the hot food.

The Reluctant Cook

Entertaining – first course

To entertain now I would begin with a first course that can be eaten with fingers or fork in front of the fire while people are finishing their pre dinner drinks. This gives me time to relax with guests if all is going well, or else retreat to titivate the main course. Favourite first courses include smoked salmon or mackerel/trout pâté – see earlier - on small biscuits/oatcakes, asparagus cooked in butter/oil in oven for 10 minutes and cheese straws.

Cheese straws

    4oz(100g) flour
    3oz(75g) butter
    2 - 3oz(50 - 75g) cheese
    1 - 2oz(25 - 50g) chopped mixed nuts or seeds
    pepper, salt and a dash of cayenne.

Rub the butter into the flour. Add the grated cheese and seasoning and mix until it all comes together – easy in an electric mixer. Roll out and sprinkle on chopped nuts/seeds. Roll lightly in then prick all over with a fork and cut into strips or rounds. Bake for 7 to 10 minutes in a hot oven.

Entertaining – main dish

This could be venison casserole, beef and horseradish or lemon and thyme lamb – anything that can be cooked in advance and will reheat well when needed. To accompany this are roast vegetables (potatoes, carrots and parsnips cut to roughly the same size, marinaded in a little oil, seasoning and chopped herbs and roasted in the oven for about 30 minutes, and greens that can be cooked quickly at the last moment.

Venison casserole

Marinade the venison for up to two days using 1 carrot, onion and stick of celery chopped and browned in a little oil and simmered for 30 minutes in 1 tablespoon wine vinegar and some red wine (amount according to budget and taste – try 1 large wine glass – add water if needed) plus 1 bay leaf and chopped garlic, rosemary and thyme. Pour over venison when cold.

To cook, drain the venison (keeping the liquid) and fry the meat quickly in a little oil and butter. Remove to a plate and fry chopped onion until brown. Sprinkle in about 1oz(25g) flour, cook then stir in the strained marinade and about ½pint (300ml) stock. Bring to the boil and add a chopped carrot, seasoning, venison and 1 tablespoon of red currant or rowan jelly. Simmer gently for about two hours or more until tender. For a party I would add more wine. If short of meat add cooked haricot beans, more vegetables (celery, mushrooms, parsnip or peppers.) Chopped herb sausages or dumplings made with bacon, suet, breadcrumbs and herbs could also be added.

Lemon thyme lamb/mutton.

Until recently we kept a few sheep which meant, having eaten the choicer cuts, we were left with various bits of uncertain age in the freezer. These I would dot with chopped garlic, rosemary and lemon thyme and roast very slowly covered in foil. When cooked and cool remove the fat and cut up the meat. Make a sauce from the residue in the roasting tin, a little flour, stock and some white wine. Add seasoning, lemon rind, lemon thyme and some milk. Add the cut up lamb/mutton and simmer for about half an hour. Remove the lemon rind and lemon thyme sprigs. Taste and add a little lemon juice, chopped lemon thyme, seasoning and extra wine as needed. Before serving add chopped parsley.

Entertaining – Puddings

Then come puddings prepared beforehand – fruit flans, fresh fruit and homemade ice cream and cheese.

Strawberry shortcake

Provide the ingredients of strawberries, shortbread biscuits and cream and guests can put together their own puddings to suit.

Shortbread

    4oz(100g) flour
    2oz(50g) rice flour or semolina
    4oz(100g) butter
    2oz(50g) castor sugar

Rub the butter into all ingredients and work together until you have a ball you can roll out, prick with a fork and cut into rounds. Bake in a cool oven for about half an hour or until pale brown. A shortbread mould (if you can find one) is useful. Dust it with flour, press the mixture in, slice off excess with knife and turn out to cook. Mark out slices whilst warm.

Glenfarclas Ice Cream

Glenfarclas is the last family owned and run independent distillery making malt whisky.

  1/2pint(300ml) double cream
  1/2pint(300ml) custard. I used to make this but now buy the best ready made.
  3 tablespoons of caster sugar
  6 tablespoons of Glenfarclas whisky
  4 to 6 teaspoons of instant coffee dissolved in a very little boiling water.

Meringues made with one egg.

First make the meringues.
   1 egg white
   2oz(50g) caster sugar

Whisk the egg white until it forms peaks – add the sugar, a little at a time, whisking well. Put spoonfuls on a well oiled or buttered tray (or use non-stick parchment paper), sprinkle on some demerara sugar and bake for 2 to 3 hours in a very cool oven. It would be sensible to make a larger amount and store the excess in a tin.

Whisk the cream until soft peaks form – then carefully fold in the custard, sugar, whisky and dissolved coffee .Break up the cold meringues roughly and stir in. Put in a container (oblong shape is useful for slicing) and put in freezer. The addition of meringues makes the ice cream easy to use straight from the freezer, as it can be cut without difficulty.

Easy Burns Night Supper

One of the least pleasant lessons at Atholl Crescent was the making of the haggis – from the very beginning. This involved putting the stomach with the heart, liver and lights in one pan and letting the windpipe hang over the side into another pan and boiling for two hours. Cut away the windpipe and mince the innards and heart adding suet, oatmeal and liquor from boiling. This mixture was then sewn into the stomach and boiled for another three hours. None of us had an appetite for haggis by the end. We also made dressed sheep's head and sheep's head broth which involved removing the brain, making little braincakes, and garnishing with sliced tongue. All of which I am sure is extremely nourishing but not something I wish to repeat.

Haggis

Nowadays haggis usually comes covered in polythene. Remove the wrapping and spread the haggis out in the bottom of the ovenproof dish. Cover and cook for ¾ of the time suggested. Meanwhile cook and mash turnip, add butter and seasoning and chopped parsley. Cook and mash potatoes, add butter, seasoning and small amount of milk. Cover haggis with mashed turnips and then the potatoes. Dot with butter and replace in the oven for 30 minutes. Serve with barely cooked shredded cabbage or salad. To save time the potatoes and turnip can be cooked and mashed together – 'turnipatoes'. Since there is no 'pudding' to ceremonially plunge a knife into, this recipe will not suit a traditional Burns night supper!

Christmas

Roast Turkey

Christmas day feast need not be difficult as nearly everything can be prepared in advance, just leaving a turkey to be roasted which if covered with foil and cooked for 30-40 minutes at a high temperature can then be left at a lower the temperature for 2 to 3 hours (according to weight) cooking again at a high temperature for the last 30 minutes without the foil. By this method a small turkey would take about 4 hours and a large one more than 6 hours. Turkeys usually come with cooking times.

Neither Christmas pudding or mince pies are popular in our family so mince pies are apple pies with a few sultanas and a sprinkling of nutmeg and cinnamon.

Cranberry Christmas pudding
 4oz(100g) butter
 4oz(100g) sugar
 6oz(175g) self raising flour
 1 or 2 apples
 2 eggs
 1oz(25g) mixed peel
 grated peel of one lemon and a little of the juice.
 1 tablespoon sherry.
 2oz(50g) cranberries.
 ½ teaspoon cinnamon (optional)

 Cream the butter and sugar until light – add the beaten eggs a little at a time beating well. Fold in the flour, apples (peeled, cored and chopped), mixed peel, grated lemon peel, sherry, cranberries, cinnamon and a little lemon juice. Put the mixture into a greased bowl, cover with a pudding cloth or foil and steam for 2 ½ hours. Freeze and steam again on Christmas day for about 1 to 2 hours. Serve with brandy butter or a sweet cranberry sauce to which you can add sherry or brandy, or port.

Cranberry sauce
    1lb(450g) cranberries
    4oz(100g) sugar
    ¼pint(150 ml) water

    Put the washed cranberries into a pan with the water and bring to the boil. Simmer until soft then add the sugar and cook very gently until the sugar has dissolved. A little orange juice can be added.

Picnics

    As a child on my father's day off we were forced to go out as we lived above the surgery and to remain there was to be called out. So we picnicked year round whatever the weather – snow, rain, fog, ice – heating soup and cooking sausages on a small methylated stove.

    Years later we set out to enjoy a pleasant picnic lunch steamboating on Loch Awe. But an unexpected storm brought sheets of rain down on our open boat. Our guests, already recovering from a car accident, were looking forlorn. We landed by the ruins of Kilchurn Castle and carried our picnic

The Reluctant Cook

Kilchurn Castle

into the one room which retained part of its roof. Tins of ready mixed gin and tonic, mugs of steaming hot salmon chowder, ham and salad rolls, richly fruited gingerbread, cheese and finally hot coffee cheered up the party fast.

The Reluctant Cook

Salmon Chowder

    1 small can of salmon or use up a left over fillet of salmon or trout

    1 onion and clove of garlic chopped

    1 stick chopped celery

    1 small tin sweetcorn

    1 pepper chopped

    1 potato and 1 carrot chopped

    herbs – parsley, dill, chervril – chopped.

    1 small tin evaporated milk

    1 pint(600ml) stock

    Sauté onion in oil/butter for a few minutes, add the other vegetables. Stir well and season. Add stock and bring to boil – simmer for about 15 minutes to cook the vegetables. Add the flaked salmon from which you have removed any bones and skin, but you can add the liquid from the tin. Add milk, sweetcorn – heat – check seasoning and lastly add chopped herbs.

    Loch Awe also brought up the problem of vegetarian barbecues. One son had failed to inform us that his girl friend did not eat meat until we were on an island with a large party and sausages, burgers and steaks sizzling on the barbecue. She had to make do with salad rolls, but I still think it is difficult even with prior knowledge. Corn on the cob and fish (in foil to avoid mixing with the meat) are probably best.

The Reluctant Cook

Scottish eggs

These are just a basic form of Scotch eggs which when homemade are delicious but take time to make and involve deep fat frying. Instead boil number of eggs required for 10 minutes. Cool and peel. Wrap in very thinly sliced ham and then in a large lettuce leaf with some herbs – basil is good. These are good for car picnics or short walks, safe in a plastic box but not good for hill walking when minimum weight is important. Then we take individually wrapped small portions of cheese and packets of oatcakes or a tin of sardines to eat with the oatcakes – biscuits dipped in fishy oil please the dog too.

Camping

Midges can make camping in Scotland miserable. Sometimes it is impossible to cook anything at all and retreat to sleeping bag with a muesli bar is the only answer!

The less time spent cooking the better so for the first evening meal potatoes, carrots and other fresh vegetables are brought ready prepared from home, cut fairly small and cooked in a little water, then cooked meat added and brought to the boil with peas or other green vegetables added last. Only one pan to wash. Vegetables will last another day in a cool box so the second evening meal will be the same but with a tin or sachet of meat. On the third day cook pasta, but drain the water before adding the tin of meat and hopefully there are some vegetables left. Celery lasts well and does not need cooking. Occasionally the sun shines with a light breeze to keep the midges away, the

The Reluctant Cook

Perfect coastal picnic

position and view are perfect and a simple meal seems like a banquet.

Healthy Eating

Healthy eating is a minefield if you listen to all the advice. Obviously it is healthy to make your main intake vegetables and fruit, followed by fish and then a small amount of meat and finally dairy produce. This is very similar to the World War II diet when an adult was rationed to 2oz(50g) butter and cheese, 8oz(225g) sugar and 4oz(100g) bacon and ham per week. Meat was rationed by availability and price (1 shilling – about £2 now.) So you can see what a lot of vegetable padding was needed. Without our own chickens (kept in a town centre back yard) we would have had to make

The Reluctant Cook

If we follow the diets for our various ailments, I'm afraid the only things we can eat are cabbage, turnips, garlic, and carrots **OR** *we could just pick all the best bits from the diets and enjoy ourselves.*

Healthy Eating

do with 1 egg a week or sometimes 1 a fortnight per person. Dried egg was available.

Although restricted this did provide a balanced diet and people were healthy. My mother certainly produced good meals from the rations available. My lack of interest in food was probably more to do with the trauma of growing up with the sound of air raids, sirens and bombs while hiding in dark cupboards and cellars. The house opposite was bombed killing all five occupants.

Sir Jack Drummond was the expert on nutrition who devised the good wartime diet for the Ministry of Food –where Marguerite Patten also worked. Sadly he was probably better known for the horrific murders of himself, wife and child whilst

The Reluctant Cook

camping in France in 1952. I remember the commotion this caused in our own household at the time—the similarities of time, place, names and ages to our own camping trips were too much to bear and we never camped in France again.

Now the press is full of wild pronouncements about food and drink. It is even worse if you are ill and see more than one doctor, each will advise on foods according to his speciality. A friend with osteoporosis was advised to eat lots of milk, cream and dairy products – advice which naturally was promptly contradicted by his heart specialist.

These are the notes I made for the student cook with some alterations for older people.

1. Eat a little meat and fish padded out with lots of vegetables (and beans, pasta, rice and potatoes for students.)
2. Eat bread – cheap – filling and nutritious if wholemeal or similar. (moderate amount for older people)
3. Eat fruit.
4. Try and find time for a good breakfast then you will not need so much at lunch when you are out having to buy ready made rolls .
5. Dried milk is useful as it can be used for adding to vegetable water to make sauces and some soups. It is also skimmed which is better for those of advanced years.

The Reluctant Cook

6. Buy celery – prices vary throughout the year but it is useful to add it chopped to any dish – it does not need cooking and is excellent nutritionally.
7. Shop, if you can, little and often for fresh foods.
8. Avoid ready prepared meals which are full of preservatives to extend shelf lives. Frozen food is better.

On the subject of healthy eating - why is food so bad in hospitals and what can be done about it? Of course the National Health Service is short of money and presumably managers take the cheapest tender regardless of quality. Is this really cost effective? A bad diet does not help people to get well quickly and release a bed. There is too much waste. It is understandable that anything not touched on the trays should be thrown out but I am told even the food on the trolleys is thrown out – surely wrapped biscuits, cakes, cheese and yoghurts could be saved. The food may be good when first cooked but a lot of it is totally unsuitable for keeping warm for any length of time. In my recent experience, fish in cheese sauce with brussel sprouts sounds good, but on taking off the lid the stench of long-kept brussel sprouts kills any appetite. The fish was so dried up it reminded me of the Norwegian fish I used to feed my dog. It would be much better to serve simple dishes that are not harmed by keeping warm. Breakfast is fine with porridge, cereal, yoghurts, fruit and bread. Lunch is also fine with soup, rolls and sandwiches but do sick people really want to be offered a corned beef and pickle sandwich? For the main meal various stews could be offered which would include carrots, celery, peas and potatoes or barley. Instead of dried up fish a

The Reluctant Cook

fish chowder would keep much better with carrots, celery, peas, potatoes, sweetcorn and parsley. Very mild vegetable curries and dahl made with split peas or lentils would also survive being kept warm. Green vegetables are not worth serving – they must loose all vitamins anyway. Mushy peas might be worth trying and salad could be served or put in the sandwiches at lunchtime. It is possible to survive on good porridge, soup, rolls and yoghurt at the moment but it would be nice to have one hot meal a day and would surely build up patients quicker.

The Reluctant Cook

Chapter 5

Baking

After years of what seemed like non-stop baking for work and family I am now happy just to bake a few things. Christmas cake, an occasional birthday cake and enough baking to give husband and myself one item with a mug of tea a day – usually scones, muffins, gingerbread or shortbread. I also make oatcakes for breakfast or lunch.

Oatcakes

    8oz(200g) oatmeal
    4oz(100g) flour
    ½ teaspoonful salt
    1 teaspoonful baking powder
    3oz(75g) butter

Rub the butter into the flour and oatmeal and add about 1 tablespoonful of cold water to make a stiff dough. Roll out on an oatmeal sprinkled board and cut into rounds. Cook for approximately 20 minutes in a moderate oven.

Manse biscuits

   8oz(225g) flour
   4oz(100g) butter
   4oz(100g) sugar
   1 egg
   ½ teaspoon cinnamon
   jam

    Rub butter into the flour. Add sugar and cinnamon. Add beaten egg and mix to a stiff dough. Knead and roll out thinly. Cut rounds and bake on greased tray for 15 minutes in a moderate oven. For my mother's family of twelve (although they only ever spent one night in the manse together before two of her brothers went to fight in the First World War) these biscuits were mostly fine on their own but for special occasions (surely that one night was one of those) they were joined together in twos with jam.

Blueberry Muffins

   6oz(175g) flour
   2oz(50g) muesli
   4oz(100g) dark brown sugar
   2 teaspoons baking powder
   ½ teaspoon salt
   2oz(50g) blueberries
   1 apple peeled and chopped - approximately 2oz(50g)
   ½ teaspoon cinnamon
   ¼ pint(150ml) milk

1/8 pint(75ml) oil
1 egg (beaten)

Mix flour, muesli, dark brown sugar, cinnamon, salt and baking powder together. Beat in the mixed egg, milk and oil and lastly stir in the apple and blueberries. Fill 8 papercases and bake for approximately 20 minutes in a hot oven. Other flavourings can be used with the basic mixture – dried fruit (sultanas) mixed spice – or chocolate.

Gingerbread
10oz(375g) flour
6oz(175g) butter
6oz(175g) dark brown sugar
1 teaspoon each of ginger and mixed spice.
2 eggs
1 small teaspoon bicarbonate of soda
1/4pint(150ml) milk
6oz(175g) sultanas
3oz(75g) chopped ginger and nuts (almonds,brasil)
6oz(175g) treacle or treacle and syrup mixed.

Slowly melt the butter, treacle and sugar. Mix flour, ginger, mixed spices and bicarbonate of soda and stir into the melted but not boiled butter mixture.

The Reluctant Cook

Beat in beaten eggs and warmed milk. Finally stir in the sultanas and half the chopped ginger and nuts. Put in two lined and greased loaf tins and scatter the remaining ginger and nuts on top. Cook for approximately 30 minutes in a moderate oven.

Girdle Scones

    8oz(225g) self raising flour
    1 ½ - 2oz(37 – 50g) butter
    pinch of salt
    1/4pint(150ml) milk
    1 teaspoon sugar
    1oz(25g) raisins, sultanas or currants.

Rub butter into flour – add other ingredients. Knead lightly on a floured board and divide into two rounds . Cut into quarters and cook on a greased girdle (or frying pan) for about 5 minutes – turn and cook other side. These can also be cooked in a hot oven for about 10 minutes. If short of bread a cheap substitute is to make these scones without the butter, sugar and fruit.

Dropped scones

    8oz(225g) self raising flour
    pinch of salt
    1 table spoon sugar
    1 dessert spoon Agave syrup

The Reluctant Cook

1 egg
just under 1/2pint(300ml) milk.

Mix together and beat in the egg and milk slowly. Grease a girdle or frying pan and drop dessert spoonfuls of the mixture on to it. When they bubble turn over and cook the other side. Keep the scones warm in a clean tea towel.

Bread

Bread sounds as if it takes a long time to make but it just involves about 15 minutes work. The rest of the time it is getting on with rising by itself. I have stayed in houses with breadmakers where warm bread is ready for breakfast. It would be an extravagance for me to buy one when it is so easy to raise the dough with an Aga. It is difficult otherwise to get the correct rising temperature. I would also miss the kneading of the dough which is very relaxing and a good way to get rid of tension. We lived long ago in a village where the head of a music college would arrive for the weekend and immediately start baking bread in order to relax. After especially stressful weeks he would be seen cycling round the village handing out his surplus loaves.

12oz(350g) strong white flour
12oz(350g) mixed wholemeal with barley, malt, wheat and barley flakes, linseed, millet or sunflower seeds – there are plenty to choose from in the shops.
2 teaspoons salt   -   mix and rub in

1oz(25g) butter   - add
1 yeast sachet   - then beat in
3/4pint(450ml) warm water
Knead for 10 minutes

Put to rise in a warm place covered with a damp clean tea towel for 1 – 1 ½ hours. Knead for a few minutes then halve and put in two warm, greased loaf tins. Put to rise again for about 30 minutes until well risen. Bake in a hot oven for 20 minutes.

For variety one half of the dough can be put back in bits in the mixer. Add 1 beaten egg, 1oz(25g) softened butter, 1 tablespoon sugar and approximately 2oz(50g) dried fruit. Mix well – if very sticky it may be necessary to add 1 or 2 tablespoons of flour. Knead for a minute then finish as above. Having mastered the basic dough one can experiment with other flours, herbs, cheese, seeds and different kinds of fruit breads.

Granny Bentinck's Fudge
    2 cups sugar
    1 cup milk
    2 tablespoons cocoa powder
    1 tablespoon butter
    4oz(100g) walnuts chopped
    2oz(50g) sultanas

The Reluctant Cook

Melt sugar, milk and cocoa slowly. Then boil rapidly for 12½ minutes. Stir in fruit and nuts and put in a greased tin. Cut when cool. I have not made this for years and found it too sweet but, as a child, after years of sweet rationing I can remember how good the crumbs tasted when I helped to cook quantities for 1950s charity sales.

The Reluctant Cook

The Reluctant Cook

Chapter 6

I began cooking with a solid fuel stove and I still cook on an oil-burning one today. Jobs involving cooking on gas or electricity did nothing to change my ideas. Solid fuel and heat storage cookers have had a bad press recently from environmentalists. But used properly they have so many extra uses eliminating the need for other appliances such as toaster, microwave, iron, tumble drier, toasted sandwich maker, bread maker, electric slow cooker, food warmer and water heater. Clothes can be aired and dried in the warm kitchen which is a magnet for family and animals. I have warmed a frozen, rejected new-born lamb in the open bottom oven – fed her and successfully re-introduced her to her mother in the morning. They are also built to last – not part of the throwaway society.

Since solid-fuel and heat storage cookers need their own style of cooking, different to gas or electric cookers, they will not suit everyone. It is essential to keep the lids closed as much as possible to conserve heat and keep consumption of fuel down. As much cooking as possible must be done in the ovens. To be economical they need to be in constant use so they are best suited to kitchens that are constantly active – cooking, preserving etc. – the kitchen of 60 years ago! Then there would have been a constant hum of activity – providing 3 meals a day cooked from scratch using vegetables and fruit in season.

J.L. Austen gives, in his memoir of his aunt Jane Austen, an idea of domestic life in her time. He says the dinners were homely 'though not less plentiful and savoury, and the bill of fare in one house would not be so like that in another as it is now, for family recipes were held in high estimation. A grandmother of culinary talent would bequeath to her descendants fame for some particular dish and might influence the family dinner for many generations.'

The Austens were almost self sufficient in food which meant Mrs Austen was probably glad to be relieved of the hard work when they moved to Bath in 1801. But there they could not even grow their own vegetables and found it expensive to buy food. They must have been glad to find a garden at their next house in Southampton where they could grow currants, gooseberries and raspberries. They moved again to Chawton and some self sufficiency again with a vegetable garden and fruit trees.

We have lost all this as, rather than families relying on what they could grow or buy locally, food travels backwards and forwards in lorries which clog up the roads. With present unemployment perhaps more people will decide to stay at

The Reluctant Cook

home, grow some food and make their own meals rather than travel to work to earn money to buy more and more processed and ready meals. It need not be as hard work as in my paternal great grandmother's time. She was self sufficient with milk, eggs, meat and vegetables but it was extremely hard work. She had a kitchen maid and parlour maid (whose book of duties I have) and doubtless a cook as well. But they needed a close eye kept on them. Manse granny as a minister's wife with ten children would have had little money. I am sure she had some help but she would have worked along with them and she certainly took a close interest in the cooking (the manse recipes are written in her hand). The large manse garden with gardener produced all the fruit and vegetables needed. My paternal grandmother kept goats and chickens in her Edinburgh garden. 'The goat is rather obstreperous and only is fairly quiet when Maud milks her.' (Extract from a letter from my great grandmother, staying with my grandmother, to her son in America in 1919.) Then life was guided more by the seasons with seasonal food, and the months marked by seasonal dishes. Fresh greens in the spring – an abundance of vegetables in the summer and in autumn a rush to preserve as much as possible for the winter. Freezers make this easy now – no need for preserving jars.

Few people have the time or place to keep animals and poultry now but growing vegetables and fruit is more easily attainable and need not be that hard work. Mrs Austen grew potatoes and advised a guest who had not eaten them before to grow her own. She replied 'No, no they are very well for you gentry but they must be terribly costly to rear.' Not so. After planting potatoes and sowing seed illness prevented me from working in my vegetable garden all summer, but it still produced bags of potatoes, sprouting broccoli, broad beans, peas, mange-tout, lettuce and a few carrots and turnips among the many weeds. The runner beans, spinach and radishes failed and I would probably have been expelled from an allotment – but it shows that things can be grown even if time is short. How much more could have been produced with just a couple of hours work a week. Vegetable gardening need not be such a time consuming chore as long as perfection is not sought and plants are kept free from choking weeds. Various vegetables can be grown among flowers – in tubs or window boxes. Blackcurrants, redcurrants, brambles, rowans, rose hips, crab apples and quince will provide fruit for eating and jams and jellies for the winter. If you have room for a tree in the garden why not make it a fruit tree? Even if you have no garden and no allotments available there may be other possibilities around. A neighbour has offered part of her too big garden to others to grow their own vegetables – a private allotment scheme.

I use a lot of herbs – they cheer up the simplest of dishes and reduce the amount of salt needed. It is essential to have quick access for cooking so I have three tubs beside the house. I grow parsley, thyme, lemon thyme, rosemary, chives, marjoram, chervil, sage, dill, oregano, bay and mint but there are many more to choose from. Mint should be grown in a bucket by itself otherwise it will take over. I do have a vegetable garden but nearer the house I keep three tubs of cut-and-come-again lettuce and four tubs of mange-tout and peas. I grow basil in the house and tomatoes in a small greenhouse. It is well worth growing herbs and lettuce as they do not take up much room in tubs or even window boxes. You can crop the cut-and-come-again lettuces many times. Rocket and small salad leaves are expensive in the shops but are easy to grow and so much better fresh when you need them. Even if you have no garden a few pots in the window will add interest to your cooking. In the winter I bring in pots of parsley, rosemary, mint and the little bay tree. Sprouting seeds are a wonderful source of vitamins and minerals, are easy to grow in the house and are delicious in salads. On a month long canal boat trip they provided us with essential fresh greens. Although using a jam jar works perfectly well it is worth buying a special sprouting jar as it makes daily watering less of a chore and more likely to be done. Due to the recent scare over sprouted seeds we have been advised to cook them thoroughly before eating. Further information and advice will doubtless appear and should be followed.

Cooking your own food and if possible growing some of it will be cheap, wholesome and give you great satisfaction. Despite Mrs Austen's hardworking life she lived until she was 88. So did my grandmothers which confirms doing so is good for you.

NOTES